Praise for
Mastering the Art of Baking with Coconut Flour

Starlene has done it again in *Mastering the Art of Baking with Coconut Flour*. She leaves no stone unturned when it comes to helping the newbie, the novice, or the experienced coconut flour baker learn how to expertly use this nutrient rich, gluten free flour. Starlene takes great care to help the reader understand how to effectively choose and use coconut flour while not bogging down the book with extraneous information. The section on how to convert a recipe from traditional flour to coconut flour is priceless! And of course there are the recipes. Oh, the glorious recipes. I get lost in the deliciousness of Starlene's creations. Trust me—you will not go wrong with any recipe in this book.

Jennifer Saleem, Hybrid Rasta Mama
http://www.hybridrastamama.com

Mastering the Art of Baking with Coconut Flour is without a doubt the most comprehensive guide to figuring out how to use this unusual ingredient with modern recipes. All of the recipes are based on real whole foods. This entire book is free of starches, sugar, and gums and with the exception of one recipe, dairy free. Whether you are new to baking with coconut flour or are an experienced baker, I guarantee that you will find this an essential, reliable, and foolproof resource. No more wasting time and expensive ingredients on recipes that turn out mediocre or, worse yet, inedible. Everything I've tried in *Mastering the Art of Baking with Coconut Flour* was a home run. Grab a copy today!

Lisa Herndon, Lisa's Counter Culture
http://www.lisascounterculture.com

Starlene Stewart is an experienced baker in traditional flours and leverages that experience master-fully in *Mastering the Art of Baking with Coconut Flour* to help you convert your own family favorite baked goods using coconut flour. Did your recipe flop? Starlene outlines the reasons and gives you the specific tools to figure out why and how to create a killer grain-free muffin the next time around.

Amanda Rose, Fresh Daily Bites
http://www.freshdailybites.com

If you've been wondering how to use coconut flour to create delicious recipes, wonder no more! Starlene takes the mystery out of baking with this grain-free flour. She doesn't simply give you her recipes that work—although she does share those, too—more importantly, she explains the proper-ties of coconut flour (and why the same recipe will work perfectly one time and the next time it won't, even with the "same" coconut flour). She doesn't just give you this key info; she actually walks you through converting grain-full recipes to grain-free recipes using coconut flour. She even includes a troubleshooting section in her book.

Shirley Braden, Gluten Free Easily

http://www.glutenfreeeasily.com

Other Books by Starlene D. Stewart

Beyond Grain & Dairy contains 113 delicious real food recipes to tantalize your taste buds, made with no grains, gluten, dairy, gums, corn, soy, or sugar. And even if you don't need to avoid any of those items, the recipes are still delicious!

Baker's Dozen Sweet Quick Breads Volume 1 in the Coconut Flour Baked Goods series includes 13 sweet quick bread recipes ranging from well loved favorites like Banana and Lemon Poppy Seed to new creations like Spiced Blackberry and Peanut Butter Chocolate Chunk.

Baker's Dozen Pumpkin Treats Volume 2 in the Coconut Flour Baked Goods series includes 13 baked goods featuring pumpkin and coconut flour, plus 8 additional recipes. You'll find several breads, waffles, an oven baked pancake, muffins, brownies and more!

Baker's Dozen Holiday Quick Breads Volume 3 in the Coconut Flour Baked Goods series includes 13 loaves of breads especially created for the winter holiday season. You'll find delights like Cranberry Orange Walnut, Chocolate Peppermint, Spiced Pear Anise Cranberry, Gingerbread, Pumpkin Maple Pecan with Streusel Topping, two Fruitcakes plus Herb Medley, a loaf you can use for sandwiches, stuffing or dressing.

Baker's Dozen Chocolate Treats Volume 4 in the Coconut Flour Baked Goods series includes 13 baked goods featuring coconut flour and chocolate, plus 11 additional recipes. You'll find several breads, a stunning three-layer chocolate cake, pudding, doughnuts, pie crust, fudge and more! Soothe your chocolate cravings with these gluten-free, grain-free and processed sugar-free treats.

Everyone Loves Pudding is an e-book of delicious raw puddings that do not include eggs, grains, gluten, dairy, gums, corn, soy, or sugar. You'll find flavors like Cherry Vanilla, Creamy Pumpkin, Silky Chocolate, Smooth Lemon, and Apple Raisin. You can have super smooth and creamy pudding again, made from real food, dairy-free, creamy, and delicious!

Winter Soups Community Cookbook is a collection of 52 soups from real food bloggers. Starlene's Crock Pot Spaghetti Sauce Soup is included along with gorgeous photos for every winter soup.

Naturally Sweetened Treats Community Cookbook is a collection of 41 sweet treat dessert recipes from real food bloggers. Starlene's Silky Chocolate Pie is included along with beautiful photos for all of the real food naturally sweetened treats.

Gluten-Free Snacks Community Cookbook is a collection of 34 gluten-free snack recipes from real food bloggers. From Appetizers to Crunchy Snacks, No Bake Sweets, and Dips, this e-book is a great place to start if you are gluten-free. Starlene's Pumpkin Poppers are included along with beautiful photos for each real food gluten-free snack.

Peace Joy Happiness: Empowerment, An Adult Coloring Book available as a paperback from Amazon.

Visit the sales site to learn more: http://www.starlene.com and sign up for the Baking with Coconut Flour newsletter for announcements: http://gapsdietjourney.com/free-conversion-pages

Mastering the Art of Baking with Coconut Flour

Tips & Tricks for Success with This High-Protein, Super Food Flour +
Discover How to Easily Convert Your Favorite Baked Goods Recipes

Starlene D. Stewart

Mastering the Art of Baking with Coconut Flour: Tips & Tricks for Success with This High-Protein, Super Food Flour + Discover How to Easily Convert Your Favorite Baked Goods Recipes Paperback Full Color Interior December 2016

ISBN: 978-1-944432-01-0

Photo Credits: Starlene D. Stewart

Front Cover Recipe: Chives and Dill Loaf

Cover Design: Vivian Cheng of Blend Creations http://www.blendcreations.com

Font: Clear Sans

Copy Editor: Victoria Hay, Ph.D. of The Copyeditor's Desk, Inc. http://www.thecopyeditorsdesk.com/

Published by HQ Productions

http://www.starlene.com

Produced in USA

Printed by Createspace

Other versions:
ISBN: 978-1-944432-02-7 Mastering the Art of Baking with Coconut Flour Paperback Black & White
ISBN: 978-0-9888263-0-4 Mastering the Art of Baking with Coconut Flour Electronic Reader Amazon Kindle

Dedication

This book is dedicated to my sons, Matthew and Kevin.

Matthew, thank you for keeping me on my toes with recipe modification requests.

Kevin, thank you for being my tech consult. I am thankful and grateful that you chose a career in information technology, I would be lost without your expertise and patience.

Acknowledgments

To my husband David, thank you for loving me and accepting me just as I am.

Disclaimer

The material in this book should be considered informational in nature and has been written for educational purposes only. As the purchaser of this book, you understand that the author is not a medical professional and that any information in this book should not be used for medical advice. The author claims no responsibility to any person or entity for any liability, loss, or damage caused or alleged to be directly or indirectly as a result of the use, application, or interpretation of the material contained in this book. Please consult your own health-care practitioner before making changes to your current diet.

Free Sample Conversion Pages

Download the Sample Conversion pages available free when you sign up for my Baking with Coconut Flour Newsletter.

As a subscriber you'll also receive coupon codes, special announcements, coconut flour baking news and tips, and best of all FREE coconut flour baked goods recipes so you can try out your new baking skills!

Enter the following URL into your browser to subscribe:

http://gapsdietjourney.com/free-conversion-pages

Contents

1. Coconut Flour - What Is It, Why Use It, and Where Can I Find it? •1
2. How Does Coconut Flour Compare to Wheat Flour? •3
3. A Comparison of Three Brand-Name Coconut Flours by Weight & Volume •5
4. Measuring: Packed vs. Sifted •9
5. Eggs, The Wildcard •11
6. Determining Desired Consistency and About Leavening Agents •15
7. Tips & Tricks for Success •17
8. Step-by-Step Recipe Conversion of Your Own Family Favorite Recipes •21
9. Recipes to Get You Started •39
10. Modification Suggestions •59
11. Troubleshooting •63
12. Coconut Flour Recipes Online •67
13. About the Author •69

Preface

When I started my health journey in December 2009, I really had no idea what I was doing. To start with, I didn't think I had any "gut" issues. But while reading The Gut and Psychology Syndrome (GAPS) book written by Dr. Natasha Campbell-Bride, I realized I did have some symptoms of gut dysbiosis, two of those being mild depression and anxiety. The GAPS Diet outlines a protocol designed to heal and seal the gut which can alleviate many symptoms, including depression and anxiety. My other aches and pains I attributed to "getting old" (*I was only 46*) and had accepted my fate. I was ready to heal my gut dysbiosis, but once that was done I figured I would simply go back to eating whatever I wanted.

After just thirteen days on GAPS, my plan turned upside down. Although I'd been diagnosed with plantar fasciitis, my feet stopped hurting and I was once again able to walk barefooted without hobbling about painfully. I could wear regular shoes without pain! Today I walk two to five miles daily with no discomfort other than some soreness on the 10,000-step days. The other major improvement was my back stopped hurting. For several years I had been unable to sleep more than seven hours without my back seizing up in pain—and I'm one of those people who needs a solid eight hours to function properly.

These two miraculous changes caused a huge paradigm shift. I was willing to stay on the GAPS Diet for as long as necessary, maybe forever, if it meant I would live without pain.

Although I was ready to give up grains forever, I missed baked goods. The GAPS Diet requires that gluten, grains, and most foods with starch are removed from the diet. Those restrictions remove many gluten-free flours leaving two: almond flour and coconut flour. I experimented with blanched almond flour first, which behaves similarly to wheat flour in that you can often get by with subbing equal parts (1:1). I loved the resulting products but wasn't totally comfortable with the high amount of almonds we were ingesting After a few recipes I decided to tackle the real challenge: coconut flour. The very first cake I ever baked using coconut flour was for my forty-ninth birthday; I adapted the Chocolate Cake[1] recipe from Elana Amsterdam's website, Elana's Pantry. It was an absolute hit with my family.

1   Stewart, Starlene D. (May 26, 2012). Recipe Review: Elana's Pantry Chocolate Cake with Coconut Flour. [Blog Post] Retrieved December 18, 2016 from http://gapsdietjourney.com/2012/05/recipe-review-elanas-pantry-chocolate-cake-with-coconut-flour/

It was a big cake, so I froze half of it to share with my coworkers (aka my Premier Taste Testers) and they loved it, too.

After that grand success, I was sold. I began to research and study this unique flour, testing it out and making other recipes. Some recipes were successful and some flopped. There wasn't a lot written about coconut flour, but in reading comments on blog posts at numerous blogs it became clear that this flour played very differently from one person to the next. What was the common link, I wondered? Pretty soon it became apparent that absorbability was a huge factor and I'll go into more of the details in this book.

Before long my creative side began to insist that I try converting some of my own recipes, even though I'd read on several sites it was best to stick with tried and true recipes. With practice, I figured out a conversion process that helped me convert recipes successfully almost every time. I wanted to share what I'd learned and *Mastering the Art of Baking with Coconut Flour* was born. Over 25,000 copies have been distributed since the release of the first edition in early 2013 and I've had many rave reviews and compliments. I'm sure you will be thrilled as well.

When I first wrote *Mastering the Art of Baking with Coconut Flour* I didn't realize what a wildcard eggs can be and how much they can affect your recipe so I've added a new chapter specifically about eggs.

Here's to your success at mastering the art of baking with coconut flour!

Starlene

Introduction

◊   Have you been interested in baking with coconut flour but have been afraid to try?

◊   Have you tried some recipes but they didn't turn out like you expected?

◊   Worse yet, you wasted expensive ingredients when the recipe flopped?

◊   Do you wonder how to make baked goods using only coconut flour and no other flours?

These questions and more are answered in this book.

I will show you how to use coconut flour to make baked goods like muffins, quick bread, sandwich bread, cookies, and brownies with some of my favorite recipes to get you started. The only flour used will be coconut flour, and real food ingredients.

In addition, you will not find any starches, gums, or sugars. I also avoid dairy products, so all but one of the recipes in this book is dairy-free (the Orange Medallion Coconut Flour Cookies contain butter). Coconut flour does work best with eggs, so you will find that all but two of the recipes include eggs—those two contain ground flax seed as the binder.

If you are able to use dairy, feel free to experiment and try substitutions; for example, use equal parts butter for coconut oil.

I also prefer to use honey over any other sweetener, so I will show you how to convert from recipes using sugar to recipes using honey. You can substitute maple syrup or agave syrup straight across for honey.

I will share some of the tips and tricks I've learned along the way, and I will show you the process I follow for converting wheat flour recipes to coconut flour so that you can try your hand at converting your own traditional family favorites.

1. Coconut Flour - What Is It, Why Use It, and Where Can I Find it?

What is coconut flour?

Coconut flour is made from the meat of the coconut. Coconut oil and coconut milk are extracted from the flesh of the coconut, leaving the flesh, which is then dehydrated, pulverized, and ground to a fine-milled flour.

Because it is made from the flesh of the coconut, it will have a light coconut flavor, but in many baked goods that flavor is masked enough that you can barely discern it. I have a couple of taste testers who hate coconut but insist they do not taste the coconut flavor in my baked goods.

Coconut flour can be different from one brand to the next. Most brands will be finely ground, similar to wheat flour, and this type works best. A few years ago I did run across one brand of coconut flour that was very fibrous and looked like minuscule pellets of coconut meat. This particular type of coconut flour will not work well with my recipes. "Homemade" coconut flour, which some folks make by drying and grinding the coconut fiber left over from making coconut milk, also will not work.

Coconut flour is gluten-free, higher in protein, and lower in carbohydrates when compared to other flours. Coconut flour also has a high fiber content.

Just a few words about fiber. The popular theory is that fiber is excellent for our bodies. However, some sources indicate that fiber is not as good for us as we've been led to believe. Fiber can, in fact, be the very cause of the problem that we are often trying to solve (most of the time we are told the cure for constipation is more fiber). To learn more on this subject, I encourage you to explore the work of Konstantin Monastyrsky, who is the author of the website called Gutsense.org. Mr. Monastyrsky is also the author of a book called Fiber Menace.

Because of the high fiber content of coconut flour, if you have a sensitive digestive system you may find that coconut flour may cause uncomfortable symptoms. So you may want to use it only occasionally, or avoid it altogether while you work to heal your gut issues and try it again after healing has occurred.

Why Use Coconut Flour?

Coconut flour can be used as a substitute when you:

◊ must avoid gluten, grains, and starches.

◊ have a sensitivity or allergy to nuts and cannot use nut flours.

◊ must avoid high oxalate foods.

Coconut flour is higher in protein and lower in carbohydrates than wheat flour, so you may find you have fewer issues with your blood sugar levels when eating products made from coconut flour.

Coconut flour tends to be filling, so you can eat less and feel satisfied longer.

Even if you don't have dietary restrictions, coconut flour presents an opportunity for new experimentation in the kitchen!

Where can I find coconut flour?

There are tutorials on the Internet that will show you how to make your own coconut flour, but I prefer to use commercially produced flour. Coconut flour can usually be found in health food stores. In many grocery stores, especially those with a health food section, you can often find Bob's Red Mill Organic Coconut Flour.

Azure Standard: (541) 467-2230   http://www.azurestandard.com

Tropical Traditions: http://www.tropicaltraditions.com

Bob's Red Mill: http://www.bobsredmill.com/organic-coconut-flour.html

Wilderness Family Naturals: https://wildernessfamilynaturals.com/collections/flours/products/coconut-flour-fiber-certified-organic-raw

Honeyville Grain: http://shop.honeyville.com/organic-coconut-flour.html

Amazon: http://www.amazon.com

Nutiva: https://store.nutiva.com/coconut-flour/

2. How Does Coconut Flour Compare to Wheat Flour?

The main difference between these two flours is that coconut flour is extremely absorbent. You will be amazed at the small amounts of coconut flour called for in most recipes. For example, a typical cake recipe using wheat flour may call for 2 cups, while the recipe using coconut flour will only call for 1/2 cup.

Another difference is that coconut flour does not contain gluten, making it a safe substitute for those who have celiac disease or are gluten sensitive.

One way that the two flours are similar is that both can be more dry or moist depending on various factors. How long has it been sitting on the shelf at the store? How has it been stored—refrigerated in an airtight container, or sitting on your counter in a container with a loose fitting lid?

I first realized that wheat flour could be moister or drier many years ago while making homemade flour tortillas. The recipe called for four cups of flour and one cup of water. One time one cup of water was exactly enough, but another time the dough would be too thick and I had to add more water. Using my own flour mill to grind wheat berries really brought to my attention the difference in the flour because the freshly milled flour had a moist texture and therefore needed even less water.

However, in my experience this problem with wheat flour did not occur very often, whereas with coconut flour it seems to happen more frequently.

Because of the high absorbency of coconut flour, I make a point to share the exact way in which I have measured my coconut flour in my recipes. My preference is to pack the flour in the measuring cup (vs. sifting and spooning lightly), and I find it's important to make sure you get an even cupful. This is accomplished by running the back of a straight-edged knife across the top of the measuring cup to get an even measurement.

You may think packing the flour and making the surface look level with a spoon or your fingers is good enough, but in using these methods I have found that there can be as much as an extra tablespoon heaped in the measuring cup. One extra tablespoon of this highly absorbent flour can easily soak up all the moisture from your recipe and make the batter drier than it should be.

You will use quite a bit less coconut flour than wheat flour; the rule of thumb is to use about one-fourth of the amount of wheat flour. For example, if your recipe calls for 1 cup wheat flour, you will be using 1/4 cup of coconut flour.

Coconut flour at first glance costs significantly more than regular wheat flour, but take into consideration that you will use much less coconut flour, which drives down the cost per serving. Most of my bread recipes use 1/2 cup of coconut flour and serve twelve or sixteen.

Bear in mind that some of the baked goods produced with coconut flour will not exactly duplicate the same items made with wheat flour. Gluten plays a huge role in the texture of the items we have grown accustomed to eating. Since coconut flour does not contain gluten, the result can be different. Some products can be reproduced successfully; for example, the Banana Nut Muffins and my Grandma's Applesauce Cake converted are so much like the original it's hard for me to tell the difference.

Most people who avoid eating gluten and grains feel so much better that they are willing to give up some favorites and are grateful when they find substitutes that are similar.

In the next chapter I'm going to compare three brand-name coconut flours to illustrate the differences in brands by volume, weight, storage factors, and product age.

3. A Comparison of Three Brand-Name Coconut Flours by Weight and Volume

To demonstrate the differences, I decided to run an experiment and weigh three different brand names of coconut flour that varied in age and methods of storage. Either factor can have an effect on the outcome of your recipe. Coconut flour is highly absorbent to start with, but if your coconut flour has dried out and lost some of its moisture, it can be even more absorbent.

The problem with this high absorbency arises when a cook's recipe calls for one cup of coconut flour. She has fashioned her recipe based upon the coconut flour in her kitchen. Let's say her coconut flour is older; this means it should be lighter in weight because it has lost moisture over time and will therefore absorb more liquids. Her recipe was created to compensate for her drier coconut flour.

Let's say your coconut flour was just shipped directly from the company and you can actually feel the moist texture. If you follow her recipe to the letter, your product will turn out to be a soggy mess and will no doubt burn before the inside is fully baked.

Or vice versa, the cook's coconut flour is fresher, therefore moister, requiring less liquid and your coconut flour is drier. In this case your batter may be so dry you can barely mix it with a spoon.

When working with coconut flour, being aware of the high absorbency factor will help ensure success in your baking endeavors. You may have tried a recipe on the Internet and could not duplicate the results, or you may have found recipes where the comments are sprinkled with feedback saying some had complete success while others did not. In my opinion, the most common reason this happens is because the coconut flour is newer or older, making it moister or drier.

If you decide to run a similar experiment and weigh your coconut flour, you may find that your coconut flour yields different weights than mine due to freshness and storage methods.

Because of these differences, your version of my recipe may not result in the same finished product. However, this is easily corrected by being aware that the amount of coconut flour I've called for in the recipe may not be the perfect amount needed for you to end up with the same end product.

When packed tightly into the measuring cup, Brand A weighs 144 grams, Brand B weighs 156 grams, and Brand C weighs 159 grams.

Brand B and Brand C were stored in sealed containers in my freezer. They are similar in weight, both relatively new purchases and stored properly. In contrast, Brand A was purchased over 17 months ago, before I started to use coconut flour regularly. It has been stored in my cupboard, and I recently came across it. I posit Brand A weighs less because it is older; in addition, it was not stored properly and has therefore lost moisture.

Coconut Flour Comparison by Weight & Volume, Packed Tightly vs. Sifted	Brand A	Brand B	Brand C
Purchased	17 months ago	9 months ago	1 month ago
Storage Method	Loosely closed bag in cupboard	Sealed container in freezer	Sealed container in freezer
Weight in grams firmly packed in 1 cup measurement	144 grams	156 grams	159 grams
Weight in grams after sifting, then lightly spooned into measuring cup	93 grams	98 grams	108 grams
1 cup firmly packed, sifted, then measured by volume	1 cup + 1/2 cup + 2 tablespoons	1 cup + 1/2 cup + 1 tablespoon	1 cup + scant 1/2 cup

We see similar differences once we sift that packed cup of coconut flour and then lightly spoon it into a measuring cup. Running a knife across the top of the filled measuring cup to make sure it is one cup evenly measured, we see that Brand A weighs 93 grams, Brand B weighs 98 grams, and Brand C weighs 108 grams.

In the last row, we see the volume for each type of coconut flour. Brand A yields 1 cup + 1/2 cup + 2 tablespoons. Brand B yields 1 cup + 1/2 cup + 1 tablespoon.

When we come to Brand C, although heaviest in weight, we find it is least in volume: once sifted and measured, it yields 1 cup + a scant 1/2 cup.

You may be asking, what is the point of this experiment again?

I am sharing this experiment to illustrate why your version of my recipe may not render the same end result.

Another factor to take into consideration, which can skew end results, is the fact that measuring vessels can hold slightly different volumes based on manufacturer. I was stunned to make this discovery! No wonder it is sometimes difficult to replicate coconut flour recipes!

In my kitchen I have three sets of dry volume measuring cups, and in comparing the 1/2 cup measurement I find the following:

Plastic: 120ml

Thin metal with spot welded handle: 125ml

Thick metal: 118ml

If the creator of the recipe uses the 118ml 1/2 cup measuring vessel and yours holds 125ml, you will end up with more coconut flour in your recipe and as a result your batter may be thicker.

This is just another factor to be aware of when reproducing others' recipes.

Be encouraged! By reading this book you will become familiar with how coconut flour behaves, your instincts around it will quickly develop, and you will create some very delicious baked goods that your family and friends are going to love!

4. Measuring: Packed vs. Sifted

Some people sift and measure coconut flour as we have sifted and measured regular wheat flour for decades; however, as you saw in my demonstration, whether you sift and measure, or pack firmly to measure (and then sift to remove clumps), makes a great deal of difference when trying to duplicate a recipe exactly.

When you sift flour, it becomes light and fluffy with air pockets. If you sift your coconut flour and lightly spoon it into the measuring cup, you may be getting much less coconut flour than the recipe you are following, if the creator of the recipe did not sift the flour. On the other hand, if you pack your coconut flour, but the creator of the recipe did *not* pack, then you will have more coconut flour than required.

It is easy enough to compensate if you do not know if the recipe calls for sifted or packed coconut flour. Simply add coconut flour in tablespoon increments to the wet ingredients, wait a minute or so for the coconut flour to absorb the liquids, and repeat, until the desired consistency is achieved.

In my experience, packing the coconut flour into the cup to measure when I share my recipes has a better chance of translating into the same end product. Bear in mind that not everyone packs their coconut flour, so pay attention to the recipe you are following to see if it specifies packing in the measuring cup, or sifting and lightly spooning into the measuring cup. If the recipe says to sift prior to measuring, the absorbency factor still comes into play (age of product, how stored, etc.), and you will likely need more or less flour to duplicate the recipe.

After packing, slide the back of a straight-edged knife across the top of the measuring cup to ensure you are getting an exact cup of flour. As explained earlier, the fact that this flour is so highly absorbent means just one extra tablespoon can make the difference between your batter being too wet or too dry (usually too dry), thereby not producing the desired end product.

Always sift your coconut flour after packing, as it tends to clump into little masses during the packing process, especially if it is newly purchased and has a moist texture.

5. Eggs, The Wildcard

When I wrote the 1st edition of this book, I had not taken into consideration the fact that eggs can be quite a wildcard. After all, they are a liquid ingredient and vary in size, especially if you are using your own backyard eggs or farmer's eggs. I've also noticed that commercially produced "large" eggs can vary in size from brand to brand.

The variables of egg size and volume became apparent to me while working with recipe testers for the first volume in my *Baker's Dozen Baked Goods Series, Sweet Quick Breads*. If you are using farmer's eggs and trying to replicate a recipe whose creator used store bought eggs you may find the recipe will need some slight adjustments.

Most recipes don't tell you the exact weight/volume of the eggs, but when you are baking with coconut flour it can dramatically change the texture of your batter as well as change the baking time. My recipe testers found more success in reproducing my recipes when I included the weight of the eggs.

Don't concern yourself with this too much; my point is to share the information so you'll be able to take this into consideration if your batter is thicker or why it had to bake longer, and how to manage it.

Size Matters

If your eggs are smaller than the recipe creator's, generally your batter will be thicker, so it will probably take less time to bake. However, if the volume of your eggs is significantly less, your batter may be too thick, so you may wish to add an egg.

On the other hand, if your eggs are larger, your batter will be thinner and the baking time may be longer than the recipe states.

According to the United States Department of Agriculture[2], one dozen "large" shelled eggs should weigh a minimum of 24 ounces or 680 grams. One egg would weigh 2 ounces, or 56.6 grams. I began

2   United States Department of Agriculture. Food Safety and Inspection Service. Shell Eggs from Farm to Table. Sizing of Eggs. (August 7, 2013). Retrieved December 18, 2016 from http://www.fsis.usda.gov/wps/portal/fsis/topics/food-safety-education/get-answers/food-safety-fact-sheets/egg-products-preparation/shell-eggs-from-farm-to-table/

weighing my eggs (without the shells) as I created each recipe and found there can be a significant difference in weight for eggs depending on various factors.

For example, did you know older eggs can weigh less? Store bought eggs are rarely as fresh as what you can get from your own backyard or your local farmer. Some sources reveal that store bought eggs can be as old as six weeks. Some folks prefer to store their farmer eggs on the countertop instead of in the refrigerator. I have no problem with that (so long as the bloom is intact[3]), but understand that unrefrigerated eggs will age faster, and part of the process of aging is dehydration of the white.

An egg fresh from the hen will weigh more than it will after it's been sitting on your countertop or even in the refrigerator for several days. Even one or two days can make a difference.

One way to test eggs' freshness is to place them in a sink of water. The newer eggs will lie at the bottom while the older eggs will float. The older the egg, the closer to the surface it will float. This is because there is an air pocket in every egg. As the egg dehydrates, the air pocket grows larger; thus older eggs float higher and closer to the surface. These eggs are usually perfectly edible, but I do make a point to crack each one open in a separate bowl just in case the egg has begun to form a chick (this is not a concern for commercially produced hens that do not reside with roosters).

Hygiene

If you purchase farmer eggs and your farmer does not wash the eggs (many do not), thus keeping the bloom intact, consider rinsing and drying your eggs just before using them.

The bloom serves a purpose of protecting the pores of the eggshell from allowing bacteria to enter, so it's really best that the farmer doesn't wash the eggs.

I suggest washing and drying eggs prior to using for two reasons.

First, consider where the egg came from. Let's face it, the production end of the hen is not exactly a sanitary opening, considering the fact that the hen voids both urine and feces from the same orifice. And if you really stop to think about it, what hen house is sanitary?

My second reason is for the times I drop a shell into the bowl while I'm cracking them open. Now my batter is contaminated. Granted my batter will bake at a high temperature, which will most likely kill any bacteria, but I prefer to maintain a sanitary batter just the same.

I prefer to wash my eggs in running water of the same temperature. For example, don't use warm water if your eggs have been in the refrigerator and are cold. Eggs are porous and this can cause

3   Scott, Brenda. (July 17, 2013). Should you wash your chicken's eggs? [Blog Post] Retrieved December 18, 2016 from http://www.wellfedhomestead.com/should-you-wash-your-chickens-eggs

bacteria on the shell to draw into the eggs. If your eggs are cold, use cold water. If they are at room temperature, use tepid water.

Temperature

I recommend using eggs (and other ingredients) at room temperature. If I've forgotten to remove the eggs from the refrigerator I will place them in a bowl of warm water for half an hour or so to bring them to room temperature.

One of the main reasons I recommend using room temperature ingredients is that I use fats such as coconut oil and cocoa butter, which will harden quickly once exposed to cold ingredients. Also, if you do use your eggs cold from the refrigerator, but the recipe you are following calls for room temperature, this can increase your baking time since the batter will need more time to heat up.

It's important to make sure the oven is at the correct temperature before placing the product inside because the eggs can separate and settle at the bottom of the loaf while the oven is heating and you could end up with scrambled egg texture at the bottom of your baked good. I usually preheat and wait to place the batter into the oven once the light indicating the temperature is correct goes off.

Purpose

Eggs work to bind the coconut flour since it does not contain gluten, the main component in wheat flour that allows the dough to stretch and spring back into place. If you find a baked good turns out moist but crumbly, try another batch using one more egg. Whole eggs and yolks contain fat, which makes the batter smooth, while beaten egg whites cause the baked good to rise. However, I find that whole eggs work best with coconut flour rather than using whites or yolks separately.

6. Determining Desired Consistency & About Leavening Agents

Determining Consistency

When baking with coconut flour, it's helpful to have experience using regular wheat flour, so you have something to compare using your own experience.

Here are some descriptions to help you determine the consistency you are trying to achieve.

◊ Cookies batter should be stiff but pliable, like typical cookie dough.

◊ Brownie batter should be thick and sticky.

◊ Quick Bread batter should be thick but soft.

◊ Cakes batter can be gravy-like.

◊ Cake batter can also have a consistency similar to quick bread, depending on your recipe.

Leavening Agents

In this book I use only baking soda and vinegar for leavening in my recipes. Baking soda needs an acid medium such as vinegar; otherwise, there will be no creation of gases, which are necessary to cause the product to rise. Other acidic mediums are buttermilk, sour cream, yogurt, and lemon juice. In addition to those ingredients, the following are also considered to be acidic[4]: chocolate, cocoa powder (not Dutch processed), honey, fruits, and maple syrup. In two of the recipes I converted, I decided to add vinegar along with the baking soda to help the product rise.

Baking soda does serve a purpose when used alone: it has the effect of helping the product brown while baking. This is known as the Maillard reaction[5].

When using vinegar and baking soda, you must be quick to mix and then immediately place your pan

4   Jaworski, Stephanie. Baking Powder and Baking Soda. Retrieved December 18, 2016 from http://www.joyofbaking.com/bakingsoda.html

5   Wikipedia. Maillard reaction. Retrieved December 18, 2016 from http://en.wikipedia.org/wiki/Maillard_reaction

of batter in the oven, because as soon as the vinegar and baking soda are mixed together they begin to produce gas[6]. The product needs to begin baking immediately so the proteins set before the gas can escape. Otherwise you may end up with a baked good that is gummy or very dense.

Eggs can also serve as a leavening agent when the eggs are whipped.

Bread that uses chemical leavening agents (i.e., baking soda, baking powder) is considered "quick" bread. Traditional or "slow" breads, on the other hand, are those produced with live leavening agents, most commonly baker's yeast.

I have never experimented with using yeast and coconut flour, although it has been done. Here are two recipes to try: Easy Healthy Yeast Bread[7] from Foodie Fiasco and Paleo Yeast Bread[8] from Paleo Plan.

---

6   López-Alt, J. Kenji. (June 21, 2010). The Difference Between Baking Powder vs. Baking Soda. [Blog Post] Retrieved December 18, 2016 from http://www.seriouseats.com/2010/06/what-is-the-difference-between-baking-powder-and-baking-soda-in-pancakes.html

7   M., Kelly. (April 15, 2013). Easy Healthy Yeast Bread. [Blog Post] Retrieved December 18, 2016 from http://www.foodiefiasco.com/easy-healthy-yeast-bread-paleolow-carbgrain-freegluten-freevegan/

8   Quinn, Neely. (December 31, 2013). Paleo Yeast Bread Recipe. [Blog Post] Retrieved December 18, 2016 from http://www.paleoplan.com/2013/12-20/new-paleo-yeast-bread-recipe/

7. Tips & Tricks for Success

Tips for Successfully Reproducing Others' Recipes

You've found a recipe on the Internet at one of your favorite blogs. The photos look amazing, the recipe seems easy enough. Unfortunately, your result looks and tastes nothing like the description or the photos. What went wrong? Here are some things to pay attention to as you follow another person's recipe.

1. Be sure to read the entire recipe carefully. I have been guilty of this myself—in my haste to make the recipe I failed to read it thoroughly, and the recipe didn't turn out. Avoid wasting expensive ingredients with this simple tip! You may also want to read the comments if the recipe is on a blog post, as you will learn from others' experience.

2. Was the coconut flour sifted or packed? Does the creator mention one way or the other?

3. Does the amount of coconut flour look like too much for the recipe? This can help you decide if the coconut flour was sifted or not. For example, most of my muffin recipes use 1/2 cup coconut flour and yield a dozen muffins. If the recipe you are looking at calls for 1 cup of coconut flour and also yields a dozen muffins, more than likely the creator of this recipe sifts and then measures. See Chapter 4 on Measuring: Packed vs. Sifted for further explanation.

4. What size is the baking vessel? This can make or break your version. Let's say the recipe creator used a 9" x 13" cake pan but you decided to use a loaf pan—when making changes like this you need to alter both temperature and cooking times. Typically a loaf needs to cook longer at a lower temperature in order to bake all the way through, whereas a flatter quick bread or cake bakes to perfection at a higher temperature, in less time.

5. As you are following the recipe, use half as much coconut flour initially when mixing it into the batter and evaluate as you go. Review Chapter 6 Determining Desired Consistency and About Leavening Agents for further explanation.

6. After you've added half the recommended amount of coconut flour, allow the batter to sit a minute or two to give the coconut flour a chance to absorb the liquids, before adding more coconut flour.

7. Does the recipe recommend bringing ingredients to room temperature? If so, don't skip this important step.

Helpful Tips

1. My recipes work best when ingredients are at room temperature. Remove your coconut flour from the freezer a few hours prior (or the night before), remove eggs from the refrigerator, and bring any other refrigerated or frozen items to room temperature.

2. Always preheat your oven. Be sure that the preheat light has turned off before placing the batter in the oven.

3. Buy yourself a good scraper spatula[9] so that you can scrape every tiny bit of batter out of the bowl. There is sometimes an entire cookie or miniature muffin's worth of batter in the scrapings from the bowl.

4. If you're making cookies or muffins, try baking one alone first. Does the cookie stay firm, or does it spread? It may need more coconut flour if it spreads instead of holds its shape. Does the muffin take too long to bake? It may need a little more coconut flour to firm up the batter.

5. Fill muffin tins to a little below the surface. Coconut flour batter needs the structure and support of the sides of the pan. Otherwise you may end up with muffins and a mushroom top that will be melded to the top of the muffin tin.

6. It is possible to substitute ground flax seed for eggs in some recipes. I have tried it with the Banana Nut Muffins and they turned out perfectly. I can't say if it will work for recipes that use more than three eggs. To make one flax "egg" you will need 1 tablespoon flax seed, freshly ground, plus 3 tablespoons of water. Place the flax meal in the bowl, stir in the water one tablespoon at a time. Allow to sit in the refrigerator 15 minutes to set up. The resulting mixture will have a texture somewhat like egg whites[10].

7. When using vinegar and baking soda as a leavening agent, mix the baking soda into the batter, and very last mix in the vinegar. Hand mix only as long as it takes to thoroughly blend the ingredients. The longer you mix vinegar and baking soda, the less likely it will be that your product will rise properly. Pour the batter into the baking utensil and immediately place in the oven—this is very important because otherwise the eggs may separate and settle at the bottom, which will result in a baked

---

9   My favorite scraper spatula from Good Cook: http://www.amazon.com/dp/B0028LZ6MG

10   Rebhal, Sayward. (October 29, 2011). How to Make a "Flax Egg" for Vegan Baking—The RIGHT Way. [Blog Post] Retrieved December 18, 2016 from http://bonzaiaphrodite.com/2011/10/how-to-make-a-flax-egg-for-vegan-baking-the-right-way/

scrambled egg texture.

8. Parchment paper works wonderfully to line baking utensils for easy removal of baked goods. When making a loaf of bread I grease the pan, then line the pan completely with parchment paper and allow the paper to stick up about 2 to 3 inches on each side to use as a handle to remove the loaf. This prevents the need to turn the loaf upside down to remove it from the pan. Some baked goods are fragile when hot, so lifting them out using parchment paper avoids the chance of the product breaking into pieces.

9. Consider investing in silicone muffin cups or loaf liners. Unlike parchment paper they can be used again and again, thus saving you money, not only because you don't have to buy replacements, but you don't waste any of your expensive ingredients!

10. Coconut flour baked goods do not rise very much, because the product is typically dense, so your leavening agents cannot do the job as easily as with lighter flours (like wheat flour). As a result it doesn't work to fill your muffin tins half full and expect a normal-sized muffin. When converting recipes, I have learned to make large enough amounts of batter to fill the baking vessel at least 3/4 of the way full.

11. Always allow the coconut flour time to absorb the liquids. I usually let the batter sit 1 to 2 minutes before adding more coconut flour.

12. If possible, use the same size baking vessel called for in the original recipe.

13. Place your loaf of bread in the center of your oven to bake. Adjust your racks if necessary.

Tips for Adapting Your Favorite Recipes

Rules of thumb I use when converting recipes:

Use 1/4 cup of coconut flour per 1 cup wheat flour (you can always add a tablespoon or two more of coconut flour, if necessary, but you can't take it out once it's mixed with liquid).

Use 1 large whole egg for every 1 ounce of coconut flour.

When the recipe includes fruit or vegetable purée, such as mashed banana or pumpkin, it is possible to use 1/2 egg for each ounce (1 large whole egg for every 2 ounces of coconut flour).

Use half as much honey in recipes calling for sugar. For example, for 1 cup sugar, use 1/2 cup honey.

If your original recipe contains sugar, and you use sugar, you can use the same amount of sugar as called for in your original recipe, and you don't need to alter the liquid amounts as you would when using honey.

In some recipes I mix together all liquid ingredients then mix in coconut flour one tablespoon at a time—allowing time for absorption—until desired consistency is achieved (this works great when making brownies).

When you need to moisten the batter, it is best to use a mixture of fats, eggs, and liquid. For example, if you are converting a cake mix, typically raw cake batter is gravy-like. Quick breads are typically thick but easy to spread. If your batter is very thick and you add 1 cup of milk, the resulting cake may not hold its shape once baked because milk isn't enough to bind the mixture. In the example above, it would be better to add 1 egg, some fat, and milk to add more liquid to the batter, rather than just milk.

I've read on the Internet that it is best to use established recipes rather than waste time and ingredients experimenting and trying to come up with your own recipes. It is true there are lots of great recipes out there already, and in the Coconut Flour Recipes Online section of this book, I will share links to sites that include coconut flour recipes.

However, I know that you probably have favorite traditional family recipes that you would love to convert. In the next section I will walk you through some recipe conversions using the steps I follow, so that you can attempt to do the same.

Note: Quick breads have been the easiest recipes to convert, so you may want to begin your experiments with your favorite quick bread recipe. I always tell people to start with the banana muffins recipe in this book as it is easy to follow and almost everyone loves banana muffins!

Each recipe conversion is an experiment! The good news is even when the result is not what you expected, it will still be edible in almost every case. Do not waste expensive ingredients! Be creative with the outcome. More than once a recipe that has not lived up to my expectations has become something else. I have even gone so far as to crumble a loaf of quick bread, add eggs and butter, mix it up, press it into a pan and bake. The outcome? Bar cookies!

8. Step-by-Step Recipe Conversion of Your Own Family Favorite Recipes

Practice Makes Perfect

Throughout my life I've found I'm more apt to pick up the process if I can see a few different examples. When reading this section please take your time and read over the process several times as this is the chapter that will help you discover how you can convert your own favorite recipes.

I've included four examples, and as you've read earlier in this book, there are factors that will vary for each cook and his or her kitchen. Your coconut flour could be moister or drier, your eggs fresher or older, or simply sized differently. But don't let that deter you from mastering the art of baking with coconut flour! Now that you have this information under your belt, you will proceed knowing what to do or what not to do.

I would like to encourage you to initially follow each recipe as written as this will help you develop your instincts around the process. Then please do begin your own experiments.

It has been my experience that most of my recipes that flopped were still edible or at least salvageable, so enjoy your baked goods.

Grandma's Applesauce Cake (Original ingredients before conversion)

1 cup sugar
2 cups sifted flour
2 large whole eggs
1 1/2 teaspoon baking soda
1 teaspoon salt
1 teaspoon cinnamon
1/2 teaspoon allspice
1 1/2 cups applesauce
1/2 cup vegetable oil
1 tablespoon vanilla
1 cup chopped dates
1/2 cup chopped pecans

Follow me as I convert this favorite childhood recipe passed down from my grandmother. I'll explain each step of the conversion.

Steps to Converting Grandma's Applesauce Cake

1. Because I use honey for sweetening, this recipe substitutes honey for the sugar.

2. Honey is twice as sweet as sugar, so I will be using 1/2 cup of honey. Much of the time I find half as much honey as sugar to still be too sweet, but I feel most safe using this modification first. If this conversion works well, I will use less honey in a subsequent test batch. I find that people who eat sugar on a regular basis prefer the converted baked goods made using the larger amount of honey, at any rate.

3. The original recipe calls for 2 cups of wheat flour. Applying the rule of thumb that you need 1/4 cup of coconut flour for 1 cup of wheat flour, I will use 1/2 cup coconut flour.

4. However, in order to more easily duplicate my recipe in the future I am going to pack my coconut flour, even though the original recipe called for sifted flour. As discussed earlier, sifting flour makes it light and fluffy with air pockets, and a measuring cup then contains less flour. Packing the flour to measure may cause my batter to be drier, so I need to keep in mind that I may need more liquids to achieve the desired consistency.

5. You need 1 egg for each ounce of coconut flour. My packed 1/2 cup of coconut flour weighs about 5 1/2 ounces, so I will round up and use 6 eggs.

6. The salt, spices, vanilla, dates, and pecans will remain the same.

7. The honey adds 1/2 cup of liquid to the recipe. Usually when converting a recipe that uses sugar

to one that uses honey, you will need to decrease your liquids. In this example, we added 1/2 cup of liquid (honey), so we would expect to decrease other liquids by 1/2 cup. However, because I am packing instead of sifting my coconut flour, I do need more liquid (wet ingredients). For this recipe I will keep the applesauce and oil in the amounts originally called for.

8. I decided to decrease the baking soda and add 2 teaspoons of apple cider vinegar.

Grandma's Applesauce Cake (Revised recipe after conversion)

This cake is light and airy, with a delicious apple and spice taste. Perfect with a cup of herb tea.

1/2 cup honey
6 large whole eggs
1 1/2 cups applesauce
1 tablespoon vanilla extract
1 teaspoon salt
1 teaspoon cinnamon
1/2 teaspoon allspice
1/2 cup coconut oil, melted
1/2 cup packed coconut flour
1 cup chopped dates (20)
1/2 cup chopped pecans
1 teaspoon baking soda
2 teaspoons apple cider vinegar

Directions

1. Grease a 9" x 13" cake pan, and line with parchment paper. Preheat oven to 350°F.

2. Add honey, eggs, applesauce, vanilla, salt, cinnamon, allspice, and melted coconut oil to a bowl.

3. Mix until well blended.

4. Measure coconut flour into a 1/2-cup measuring utensil, packing firmly. Use the back side of a knife to cut across the top of the measuring utensil so that your measurement is exactly 1/2 cup. Sift flour to remove any lumps.

5. Mix half of the coconut flour in with the wet ingredients. Allow to sit for 2 minutes to give the coconut flour time to absorb. You are looking for a soft, fluffy texture.

6. Add more coconut flour until you reach the desired consistency.

7. Add baking soda, dates, and nuts; mix briefly by hand. Add apple cider vinegar; mix briefly by hand just until combined.

8. Pour batter into cake pan; spread to edges using a scraper spatula. Bake 30 minutes or until a toothpick inserted comes out clean.

Recipe Conversion 2—Whole Wheat Banana Nut Muffins

Banana Nut Muffins (Original ingredients before conversion)

1 cup mashed bananas
1/3 cup oil or butter
1/2 cup honey or brown sugar
2 large whole eggs, beaten
1 3/4 cup whole wheat flour
1/2 teaspoon salt
1 teaspoon baking soda
1/4 cup hot water
1/2 cup chopped nuts

Steps to Converting Banana Nut Muffins

1. The rule of thumb is to use 1/4 cup of coconut flour for every cup of wheat flour. In this case, instead of solving algebraic equations to calculate exactly how much coconut flour to use, I just went with a straight 1/2 cup. (For the record, it would have been 7 tablespoons of coconut flour).

2. To more easily duplicate my recipe in the future, I am going to pack my coconut flour.

3. Since this recipe includes mashed bananas, I used 1/2 egg per 1 ounce of coconut flour.

4. The salt, oil, and nuts will remain the same.

5. I omitted the water.

6. I am adding 2 teaspoons of apple cider vinegar to help the muffins rise.

These muffins, in my opinion, are actually a little too sweet, so next time I will try halving the honey.

Banana Nut Muffins (Revised recipe after conversion)

Light and airy. I advise starting with these if you are new to baking with coconut flour. Almost everyone loves banana muffins.

1/2 cup coconut flour, packed
1 cup bananas, mashed
1/3 cup melted coconut oil
1/2 cup honey
3 large whole eggs
1/2 teaspoon sea salt
1/2 teaspoon baking soda
2 teaspoons apple cider vinegar
1/2 cup walnuts, chopped

Directions

1. Preheat oven to 350°F.

2. Place cupcake papers into muffin tins, or grease liberally and dust using coconut flour, or use silicone inserts.

3. In a mixing bowl, mash bananas until creamy, and stir in honey. Melt coconut oil and whisk in. Add eggs, salt and baking soda. Blend using a hand mixer or whisk.

4. Measure coconut flour into a 1/2-cup measuring utensil, packing firmly. Use the back side of a knife to cut across the top of the measuring utensil so that your measurement is exactly 1/2 cup. Sift flour to remove any lumps.

5. Mix half of the coconut flour in with the wet ingredients. Allow to sit for 2 minutes to give the coconut flour time to absorb. You are looking for a consistency of mashed potatoes. If the mixture is runny, add the rest of the coconut flour. Again allow batter to sit for 2 minutes.

6. Add walnuts and vinegar, stir by hand.

7. Fill 12 cupcake forms (slightly under filled). Bake for 25 minutes or until lightly browned on top and a toothpick inserted comes out clean.

I have also tested this recipe using "flax egg" in substitution for the eggs. You will need 3 tablespoons of flax seed plus 9 tablespoons of water. Grind the flax seed fresh each time as it degrades quickly once ground. Place the flax meal in the bowl, and then stir in the water one tablespoon at a time. Allow to sit in the refrigerator 15 minutes to set up. The resulting mixture will have a texture somewhat like egg whites.

Tip: Always preheat your oven. Be sure that the preheat light has turned off before placing batter in the oven.

Recipe Conversion 3—Brownies

Brownies (Original ingredients before conversion)

3 ounces semisweet chocolate chips
1/2 cup carrot purée
1/2 cup spinach purée
1/2 cup firm packed light brown sugar
1/4 cup cocoa powder
2 tablespoons margarine
2 teaspoons vanilla
2 large whole eggs
3/4 cup all purpose flour
1/2 teaspoon baking powder
1/2 teaspoon salt

Steps to Converting Brownies

In this recipe I used a completely different method, which worked out quite well—I added the wet ingredients together first, and then mixed in coconut flour one tablespoon at a time.

1. I omitted the spinach purée and used only carrots (you would NEVER guess there are carrots in these brownies).

2. Initially I used 1/4 cup of honey (4 tablespoons), but the original recipe called for semisweet chocolate and I used Baker's chocolate, which is unsweetened. I let my taste guide my decision to add 2 more tablespoons of honey.

3. I substituted coconut oil for the margarine; butter would work nicely as well.

4. I omitted the baking powder and did not substitute a leavening agent as brownies typically don't rise much, if at all, and they don't need to brown in order to look done.

5. I mixed all of the wet ingredients together, plus the salt and cocoa powder.

6. Then I added coconut flour, one tablespoon at a time, until the consistency was thick and sticky, as raw brownie batter should be. Two tablespoons of coconut flour was all that was needed to thicken the batter to the desired consistency.

7. I added walnuts to the revised recipe.

Brownies (Revised recipe after conversion)

These brownies are dense and very rich in chocolate.

1 cup cooked carrots (about 3 carrots)
3 large whole eggs
3 ounces Baker's unsweetened baking chocolate squares (100% cacao)
1/4 cup coconut oil
6 tablespoons honey
1/4 cup cocoa powder
2 teaspoons vanilla extract
2 tablespoons coconut flour, packed
1/2 teaspoon salt
1/2 cup walnuts, chopped

Directions

1. Grease an 8" x 8" glass baking dish with coconut oil.

2. Place three carrots in a steamer and cook until tender, about 25 minutes. Allow to cool to room temperature.

3. Melt chocolate squares in a double boiler over low heat. If you don't have a double boiler, just place a glass Pyrex or oven-safe bowl over a small pan of water. It will take about 15 minutes to heat the water and melt the chocolate until it is liquefied.

4. Add the coconut oil in with the chocolate squares to melt. Preheat oven to 350°F.

5. Place 2 eggs and cooled carrots in your blender and process until puréed. Pour this mixture into a medium-sized mixing bowl.

6. Add remaining egg, honey, cocoa powder, vanilla extract, and salt to the mixture. When the chocolate squares and coconut oil are melted and slightly cooled, add them to the ingredients in the mixing bowl. Mix together.

7. The mixture should be creamy, like pudding. Add 1 tablespoon of coconut flour at a time and mix thoroughly, waiting 2 minutes before adding more to allow the coconut flour to absorb the liquids. You are looking for a thick, sticky batter.

8. Spread the batter into the 8" × 8" glass cooking dish.

9. Bake for 20 minutes or until internal temperature reaches 160°F and brownies are firm to the touch.

Tip: Buy yourself a good scraper spatula so that you can scrape every tiny bit of batter out of the bowl. There is sometimes an entire cookie or mini-muffin's worth of batter in the scrapings.

Recipe Conversion 4—Pumpkin Poppers (Doughnut Holes)

Pumpkin Poppers (Original ingredients before conversion)

1 3/4 cups all-purpose flour
2 teaspoons baking powder
1/2 teaspoon salt
1/2 teaspoon cinnamon
1/2 teaspoon nutmeg
1/2 teaspoon allspice
1/8 teaspoon ground cloves
1/3 cup vegetable oil
1/2 cup brown sugar
1 egg
1 teaspoon vanilla extract
3/4 cup canned plain pumpkin
1/2 cup low-fat milk

Steps to Converting Pumpkin Poppers

1. The rule of thumb is to use 1/4 cup of coconut flour for every cup of wheat flour. This recipe called for 1-3/4 cup as did the Banana Nut Muffins, and I decided on using 1/2 cup coconut flour (instead of exactly 7 tablespoons).

2. To more easily duplicate my recipe in the future, I am going to pack my coconut flour.

3. Since this recipe includes pumpkin, I used 1/2 egg per ounce coconut flour and will use 3 large eggs.

4. I omitted the baking powder; I do not use it in my cooking as it contains cornstarch and I do not use corn products. Also, I suspected this baked good would not rise much and so I decided against using any leavening ingredients.

5. I decided to double the amount of cinnamon and nutmeg, and cloves. The allspice remained the same, and I added ginger, which is optional.

6. I substituted coconut oil for the vegetable oil straight across.

7. For the 1/2 cup of brown sugar I used half as much honey, 1/4 cup.

8. The vanilla extract remains the same.

9. I increased the 3/4 cup of pumpkin to 1 full cup. I also decided to include 1/2 cup carrots along with the pumpkin in my recipe to make the Pumpkin Poppers a brighter orange color.

10. I omitted the low-fat milk altogether because I figured the honey was a liquid and I added 1/4 cup more pumpkin.

The original recipe from which I converted can be found on the Internet here:

http://cravingchronicles.com/2010/10/11/baked-pumpkin-spice-donut-holes/

Pumpkin Poppers (Revised recipe after conversion)

1/2 cup coconut flour, firmly packed
1/2 teaspoon sea salt
1 teaspoon + 1/2 teaspoon ground cinnamon, divided use
1/4 teaspoon nutmeg
1/2 teaspoon allspice
1/4 teaspoon cloves
1/4 teaspoon ginger (optional)
3 large whole eggs
1/2 cup cooked pumpkin and 1/2 cup carrots (or you can use 1 cup butternut squash)
1 teaspoon vanilla
1/3 cup virgin coconut oil + 1 tablespoon coconut oil, divided use
1/4 cup + 1 tablespoon honey, divided use

Directions

1. Be sure to get an exact 1/2 cup of coconut flour by using the back of a straight edged knife to level off the flour even with the top edge of the measuring cup. Sift to remove clumps.

2. Set aside several tablespoons of coconut flour.

3. Place remaining coconut flour and other dry ingredients (spices and salt) in a large mixing bowl.

4. Whisk dry ingredients together to thoroughly blend spices.

5. Place 3 eggs into your blender or food processor with the pumpkin and carrots (or squash) and blend until completely smooth.

6. Place melted coconut oil, honey, and vanilla into a small bowl.

7. Mix the vegetable and egg mixture in with the oil, honey, and vanilla and whisk together.

8. Add wet ingredients to dry ingredients (keeping the reserved coconut flour to the side).

9. Using a hand mixer, blend for 1 or 2 minutes until completely mixed. As the coconut flour absorbs the liquids the mixture will change from having a soup-like consistency to a thicker consistency.

10. Allow the batter to sit for 2 minutes, so that the coconut flour can absorb the liquids.

11. The batter should be firm enough to allow you to pick it up in your hands and form into a little ball.

Add remaining coconut flour as needed until you reach this consistency.

12. Preheat oven to 325°F.

13. Use coconut oil to grease a mini-muffin tin. Lightly sprinkle coconut flour into the bottom of each muffin cup. Measure out 2 tablespoons of batter for each popper. Form a small round ball with the dough.

14. Drop into the greased and floured muffin tins. I don't advise using cupcake papers for this recipe (you may, although the batter melds into the creases and your end product resembles a mini-muffin rather than a round "doughnut hole").

15. Bake for 20 minutes.

TOPPING: Mix 1 tablespoon melted coconut oil with 1 tablespoon honey and 1/2 teaspoon ground cinnamon.

When poppers are done, immediately drizzle 1/4 teaspoon of the topping mixture on each popper. The topping will melt into the popper and down the sides, soaking into the bottom.

NOTE: Carrots will give the poppers more of an orange color. In this recipe I used half pumpkin and half carrots so that the poppers would be more orange-colored. You can use all butternut squash, all pumpkin, all carrots or a combination.

9. Recipes to Get You Started

Orange Medallion Cookies

Yield 24 cookies

These cookies are soft with a delicate orange flavor.

1/2 cup honey
1/2 cup room temperature butter (soft)
1/2 cup coconut flour, packed
3 large whole eggs
1 teaspoon orange zest
1/2 teaspoon salt
1/2 teaspoon vanilla extract
vanilla bean caviar from 3" vanilla bean (optional)

Directions

1. Preheat oven to 350°F.

2. Measure coconut flour; set aside 1/4 cup. Place all ingredients in a bowl and mix thoroughly with a mixer until well blended, a minute or two.

3. Allow to sit for 2 minutes so that the coconut flour can absorb the moisture. Add more coconut flour until cookie dough is soft and pliable.

4. Drop the batter onto a greased cookie sheet by measured, even tablespoonfuls. Butter your fingers lightly and pat and tap the cookie into a round shape.

5. Bake for 8 minutes. When done, cookies will lose their glossy look.

6. If you press lightly on the cookie and it leaves an indent, return to the oven for another 2 or 3 minutes to finish baking.

You can find the Buttercream Frosting recipe at: http://www.modernalternativemama.com/blog/2012/04/05/recipe-collection-refined-sugar-free-vanilla-buttercream/

Strawberry Shortcake Medallion Cookies

Yield 24 cookies

These cookies are soft with a lovely strawberry flavor.

1 pound of strawberries, stems removed, cored, and sliced thin
1/3 cup and 1 tablespoon coconut oil, divided use
1/2 cup and 2 tablespoons coconut flour
1/3 cup honey
2 large whole eggs
1/2 teaspoon vanilla extract
vanilla bean caviar from 3" vanilla bean, optional

Directions

1. Rinse and clean 1 pound of strawberries. Remove the stems and cores, and slice thinly. In a pan with a thick bottom, melt one tablespoon coconut oil.

2. Add the strawberries. Bring to a boil and reduce heat so that the strawberries are simmering. Stir regularly—about every five minutes. Simmer on low heat until strawberries have reduced to 1/2 cup of jam, about 50 to 60 minutes.

3. Allow the strawberry jam to cool thoroughly before proceeding to the next step.

4. Pack coconut flour into a 1/2-cup measuring cup, being sure to scrape off the excess with a straight knife. Sift coconut flour to remove lumps.

5. Set aside several tablespoons of coconut flour.

6. Place the remaining coconut flour into the bowl, along with the 1/2 cup coconut oil, eggs, honey, vanilla, and vanilla bean caviar. Whip with a hand mixer until mixed well.

7. Allow batter to sit for 2 minutes to allow coconut flour to absorb the liquids. Add remaining coconut flour in increments until you have a soft dough that can be formed into a ball that holds its shape.

8. Place cooled strawberry jam in with the cookie dough and lightly stir to create a swirled effect.

9. Preheat oven to 325°F. Lightly grease a cookie sheet. Drop by level tablespoons onto the cookie sheet.

10. Moisten fingertips with coconut oil—lightly pat and tap the cookie dough into a round shape.

11. Bake for 10 minutes. Cookies lose their shiny look when done and will feel firm to the touch.

12. If pressing lightly leaves a dent, return to oven and bake 1 or 2 more minutes until done.

Chocolate Medallion Cookies

Yield 36 cookies

1/2 cup honey
1/2 cup coconut oil
1/2 cup + 2 tablespoons coconut flour, packed
1/2 cup cocoa powder
4 large whole eggs
1/2 teaspoon salt
1/2 teaspoon vanilla extract

Directions

1. Preheat oven to 350°F.

2. Add honey and coconut oil together in a small pan and heat until warm and melted.

3. Measure coconut flour into a 1/2-cup measuring utensil, packing firmly. Use the back side of a knife to cut across the top of the measuring utensils so that your measurement is exactly 1/2 cup. Sift flour to remove any lumps.

4. Place cocoa powder, eggs, salt, and vanilla into a bowl. Once honey and coconut oil are melted, add to bowl.

5. Beat with a mixer until well blended.

6. Mix half of the coconut flour in with the wet ingredients. Allow to sit for 2 minutes to give the coconut flour time to absorb. The batter will be moist but easily formed into a ball.

7. Add more coconut flour until you reach the desired consistency.

8. Measure even tablespoons and drop onto a cookie sheet greased with coconut oil. These cookies will not increase much in size, if at all, since there is no leavening agent, so you can put them pretty close together.

9. Once you have them all measured out, dip your fingers into the coconut oil and tap and pat the cookie dough into a flat round medallion.

10. Bake for 8 minutes and check. These cookies lose their shiny appearance and will feel firm to the touch when done. If they are not quite done, you will be able to touch them lightly and leave a dent, so let them bake another minute or two.

Cookie Cutter Cookies

Yields 10 snow people

These cookies are so much fun! I just loved the process of making "clothing" for each snowperson.
Note: Make your vegetable leather first if you plan to dress your snow people (recipe follows).

1/2 cup coconut oil, solid
1/4 cup honey
1 large whole egg
2 teaspoons orange zest (about 2 medium oranges)
1/8 teaspoon cloves
1 teaspoon vanilla
1/2 cup coconut flour, packed
Fruit or vegetable leather (for decorating, if desired)

Directions

1. Preheat oven to 350°F.

2. Place 1/2 cup solid coconut oil in a bowl. Add 1/4 cup honey. Beat with mixer until whipped. Add egg, orange zest, cloves, vanilla and mix.

3. Measure 1/2 cup of coconut flour, firmly packed. Run the back of a knife to cut across the measuring cup to be sure you get an even measurement. Sift the flour to remove any small clumps. Reserve several tablespoons of coconut flour.

4. Place the remaining coconut flour into the bowl with the wet ingredients and mix thoroughly with a hand mixer. Allow to sit 2 minutes so the coconut flour can absorb the liquids. If the dough is stiff but pliable and can be formed into a ball of dough, don't add any more coconut flour. Otherwise, add more and allow to sit 2 minutes to absorb moisture.

5. Form dough into a ball. The texture should be very much like typical wheat-based cookie cutter cookie dough. Divide ball in half. Place each half between two pieces of parchment paper and flatten into a circle. Refrigerate 15 minutes (not any longer, because the dough will become too stiff).

6. Remove from refrigerator and roll the dough slightly thinner with parchment paper in place. If dough has gotten too stiff to easily roll out, allow to sit at room temperature for a few minutes.

7. Cut into snowpeople using cookie cutters. Apply "clothing" before baking.

8. Bake for 7 minutes.

Please visit my guest post at Delicious Obsessions: http://www.deliciousobsessions.com/2012/12/grain-free-cookie-cutter-cookie-recipe-gluten-grain-and-dairy-free/

Egg-Free Cookie Cutter Cookies

1/2 cup coconut oil, solid
1/4 cup honey
1 tablespoon sprouted flax seeds
3 tablespoons water
2 teaspoons orange zest (from about 2 medium oranges)
1/8 teaspoon ground cloves
1 teaspoon vanilla
1/2 cup coconut flour, packed
Fruit or vegetable leather (for decorating, if desired)

Directions

1. Preheat oven to 350°F.

2. Grind sprouted flax seeds until they are as fine as flour. I use my Magic Bullet with the low blade, but any blender or food processor should work. Place the flax meal in a small bowl and then stir in the water one tablespoon at a time. Allow to sit in the refrigerator 15 minutes to set up. The resulting mixture will have a texture somewhat like egg whites.

3. Place 1/2 cup solid coconut oil in a bowl. Add 1/4 cup honey. Beat with mixer until whipped. Add orange zest, cloves, vanilla and flax "egg" and mix.

4. Measure 1/2 cup of coconut flour, firmly packed. Run the back of a knife to cut across the measuring cup to be sure you get an even measurement. Sift the flour to remove any small clumps.

5. Reserve several tablespoons of coconut flour.

6. Place the remaining coconut flour into the bowl with the wet ingredients and mix thoroughly with a hand mixer. Allow to sit 2 minutes so the coconut flour can absorb the liquids. If the dough is stiff but pliable and can be formed into a ball of dough, don't add any more coconut flour. Otherwise, add more and allow to sit 2 minutes to absorb moisture.

7. Form into a ball. The texture should be very much like typical wheat-based cookie cutter cookie dough. Divide ball in half. Place each half between two pieces of parchment paper and flatten into a circle. Refrigerate 15 minutes (not any longer, because the dough will become too stiff).

8. Remove from refrigerator and roll the dough slightly thinner with parchment paper in place. If dough has gotten too stiff to easily roll out, allow to sit at room temperature for a few minutes.

9. Cut into snowpeople using cookie cutters. Apply "clothing" before baking.

10. Bake for 7 minutes.

Beet and Carrot Vegetable Leather

I was so thrilled with the cute "clothing" I made for the snow people. Looking at the photos brings a smile to my face. Just look at the adorable hats and the cute apron on the snow woman! It's a super bonus that the "clothing" is homemade with vegetables, so no sugar, food coloring or weird ingredients! The colors are beautiful, I hope you try making some to decorate your snow people. :-)

2 medium beets
5 peeled carrots
2 apples
2-4 T. honey, optional

Directions

Note: Steam beets and carrots separately to prevent the beets from staining the carrots.

1. Steam beets and one apple in a saucepan for 45 minutes or until fork tender.

2. Steam carrots and the other apple in second saucepan for 25 minutes or until fork tender.

3. Remove from heat and allow to cool to room temperature.

4. Blend beets and apple, adding one tablespoon of water at a time until they are an applesauce-like purée. If desired, sweeten to taste using 1-2 tablespoons of honey. Bear in mind as the leather dries it will taste sweeter.

5. Do the same with the carrots and apple.

6. Spread purée onto greased fruit roll sheets until very thin, about 1/8".

7. Place in dehydrator at 140°F and dry for 8-20 hours. Test for dryness by touching the center of the leather; no indentation should be evident and no "wet" spots should show.

8. Cut pieces of leather into desired shapes and apply to decorate the cookies—before baking.

Pumpkin Bread

1 3/4 cup cooked pumpkin (or butternut squash/winter squash)
1/2 cup coconut oil, melted
1/2 cup honey
6 large whole eggs
1 cup raw carrots, peeled, shredded and riced (3 large carrots)
1/2 cup coconut flour, packed
1 teaspoon sea salt
1 teaspoon ground cinnamon
1/2 teaspoon ground nutmeg
1/8 teaspoon ground allspice
1/8 teaspoon ground cloves
1 teaspoon baking soda

Directions

1. Preheat oven to 325°F.

2. Grease a glass loaf pan 8.5" x 4.5" x 2.5" (1.5 quart) and line with parchment paper. Lightly grease the parchment paper. This makes removing the loaf simple and ensures that it will remain intact.

3. In a large mixing bowl place pumpkin (or squash), coconut oil, honey, and eggs. Using a mixer, blend until all ingredients are mixed together thoroughly.

4. Peel carrots. Shred, then mince into tiny pieces, similar to rice. Add the raw carrot bits to the wet ingredients. Add the spices, baking soda, and salt to one bowl. Whisk together so the spices are mixed throughout.

5. Reserve several tablespoons of coconut flour. Add the remaining coconut flour to the dry ingredients and mix.

6. Add the dry ingredients to the wet ingredients, using your mixer blend together until thoroughly mixed. The mixture will thicken as the coconut flour absorbs the fluids. Allow mixture to sit for 2 minutes. Add remaining coconut flour in increments, until you have a soft but thick batter.

7. Add the baking soda and mix briefly. Spoon the batter into the loaf pan and smooth the top. Ideally your batter fills the loaf pan right to the top. It will rise just a small amount, about 1/2".

8. Bake for 1 hour and 10 minutes or until browned on top and a toothpick inserted comes out clean.

9. Remove from oven and allow to rest about 10 minutes before carefully removing to a cooling rack.

Sandwich Bread

This sandwich bread is best sliced thin, great toasted, and amazing for breakfast as French toast served with honey and butter. It is dense and similar in texture to old-fashioned white bread.

12 large whole eggs
3/4 cup coconut oil, melted
3 tablespoons honey
1/2 cup coconut flour, packed
3/4 teaspoon sea salt
1/2 teaspoon baking soda
2 teaspoons apple cider vinegar

Directions

1. Preheat oven to 325°F. Be sure oven is preheated to the correct temperature.

2. Grease a loaf pan and line with parchment paper for complete ease in removal of loaf when done.

3. In a large mixing bowl, combine eggs, melted coconut oil, honey, and salt. With an electric mixer, mix at low speed until all ingredients are fully incorporated.

4. To measure the coconut flour, pack firmly into the cup measurement and use the back of a straight knife to level the flour even with the top edge of the measuring cup.

5. To ensure there are no lumps, sift flour.

6. Begin by adding half of the coconut flour into the egg mixture. Blend until well mixed and allow to sit for 2 minutes. If the batter is extremely runny (like gravy), add the remaining coconut flour. Otherwise add 1 tablespoon at a time until you get a texture that is somewhat fluffy but not as runny as cake mix batter. It's better to add flour in small amounts until you find the correct texture than to compensate by adding more liquids and fats.

7. Allow to sit for 2 minutes to allow the coconut flour to absorb liquids. Add baking soda and mix together quickly. Add vinegar and hand stir just long enough to mix it in thoroughly (2 or 3 seconds).

8. Pour immediately into the bread pan and place in a preheated oven. Bake 40 minutes. Lightly cover with a tent of aluminum foil and bake for 10 more minutes.

9. Loaf will feel firm to the touch when done.

Faux Cornbread or Muffins

This cornbread recipe relies on butternut squash to give it the characteristic deep yellow of cornmeal. Delicious sliced, as muffins, and also works great for cornbread stuffing.

10 large whole eggs
1/2 cup butternut squash
1/2 cup coconut oil, melted
3 tablespoons honey
1/2 cup coconut flour, packed
3/4 teaspoon sea salt
1/2 teaspoon baking soda
2 teaspoons apple cider vinegar

Directions

1. Preheat oven to 350°F. Grease a shallow brownie pan (11" x 7") and line with parchment paper for complete ease in removal of loaf when done. This will be a flat loaf, about 1" in height.

2. Place 2 eggs and butternut squash into your blender. Process until completely smooth. Place the mixture into a large mixing bowl. Add the remaining eggs, melted coconut oil, honey, and salt. Mix on low until combined.

3. To measure the coconut flour, pack firmly into the cup measurement and use the back of a straight knife to level the flour even with the top edge of the measuring cup.

4. To ensure there are no lumps, sift coconut flour.

5. Add 1/4 cup of coconut flour to the egg mixture. Blend until well mixed and allow to sit for 2 minutes. If the batter is extremely runny (like gravy), add the remaining half of the coconut flour. Otherwise add 1 tablespoon at a time until you get a texture that is somewhat fluffy but not as runny as cake mix batter. It's better to add flour in smaller amounts until you find the texture you want than to compensate with adding more liquids and fats.

6. Allow to sit for 2 minutes to allow the coconut flour to absorb liquids. Add baking soda and mix together quickly.

7. Add vinegar and mix just long enough to mix it in thoroughly (2 or 3 seconds). Immediately pour into the baking dish and place in the preheated oven.

8. Bake for 30 minutes. The cornbread will be lightly browned and firm to the touch. You could try using an 8" x 8" pan for a taller end product. Be aware that baking time may increase.

Recipe variation: This recipe also makes one dozen cornbread muffins. Bake for 15-20 minutes.

Zucchini Tomato Flat Bread

We like to eat this flat bread with chili, and it would make an awesome pizza crust! Bake first, then add toppings and pop back into the oven for about 15 minutes at 400°F. Yummy!

2 tablespoons coconut flour, packed
2 large whole eggs
8 ounces unpeeled zucchini squash, shredded
1 Roma tomato, diced
1 clove garlic, crushed
1/2 teaspoon salt
1/4 teaspoon black pepper

Directions

1. Preheat oven to 325°F.

2. Grease a pizza pan or cookie sheet then line with parchment paper. Lightly grease the parchment paper. The parchment paper is very important as the flat bread will stick.

3. To measure the coconut flour, pack firmly into the tablespoon measurement and use the back of a straight knife to level the flour even with the top edge of the measuring spoon.

4. To ensure there are no lumps, sift the coconut flour.

5. Place coconut flour and eggs into a bowl and mix.

6. Mix in zucchini squash, tomato, garlic, salt, and pepper.

7. Allow to sit for 2 minutes to allow the coconut flour to absorb liquids.

8. The batter will be wet and slightly runny.

9. Place batter onto parchment paper and smooth into a large flat round using the back of a spoon.

10. Bake for 30 minutes on one side.

11. Remove from oven and flip to the other side.

12. Bake 30 more minutes.

In order to flip the flat bread to the other side I usually place a piece of parchment paper on the flat bread, then use a pizza peel to lay on top and flip.

If your zucchini seems to have an extreme amount of moisture you may wish to squeeze in a kitchen towel to remove some of the fluid. Adding a small amount of coconut flour to absorb the liquid is also an option.

Chives and Dill Loaf

This loaf is excellent for making sandwiches. It slices perfectly and holds together very nicely.

9 large whole eggs
1/2 cup coconut oil, soft or melted
2 tablespoons honey
3/4 teaspoon sea salt
1/4 teaspoon black pepper
1/2 cup coconut flour, packed
1 tablespoon fresh dill leaves or 1 teaspoon dried
1 tablespoon fresh chives or 1 teaspoon dried
1/2 teaspoon baking soda
2 teaspoons apple cider vinegar

Directions

1. Preheat oven to 325°F. Be sure oven is preheated to the correct temperature.

2. Grease a loaf pan and line with parchment paper for complete ease in removal of loaf when done. Use a piece large enough so the sides can be used as handles to remove the loaf.

3. Cut fresh chives into 1/2" pieces.

4. In a large mixing bowl, combine eggs, melted coconut oil, honey, salt, and black pepper. With an electric mixer, mix at medium speed until all ingredients are fully incorporated.

5. To measure the coconut flour, pack firmly into the cup measurement and use the back of a straight knife to level the flour even with the top edge of the measuring cup. To ensure there are no lumps, sift flour.

6. Begin by adding half of the coconut flour into the egg mixture. Blend until well mixed and allow to sit for 2 minutes. If the batter is extremely runny (like gravy), add the remaining coconut flour. Otherwise add 1 tablespoon at a time until you get a texture that is soft but holds its form. It's better to add flour in small amounts until you find the correct texture than to compensate by adding more liquids and fats.

7. Allow to sit for 2 minutes to allow the coconut flour to absorb liquids.

8. Add chives and dill, hand mix with a spoon. Add baking soda and hand mix together quickly. Add vinegar and hand mix just long enough to mix it in thoroughly (2 or 3 seconds).

9. Pour immediately into the bread pan and place in a preheated oven. Bake 55 minutes.

10. Loaf will feel firm to the touch when done. When you press on the loaf, pay attention to feeling of

firmness at the sides, compared to the center. Typically the outer crust will be done, but in order to avoid the dreaded ball of raw dough in the center, the center of the loaf needs to feel as firm as the sides.

11. Once loaf is done, use the parchment paper "handles" to remove from the pan. Place on a rack to cool.

10. Modification Suggestions

Cookies

The following three cookie recipes were all modified from the same original recipe.

Orange	Strawberry	Chocolate
1/2 cup honey	1/3 cup honey	1/2 cup honey
1/2 cup butter	1/2 cup + 1 T. coconut oil	1/2 cup coconut oil
1/2 cup coconut flour	1/2 cup + 2 T. coconut flour	1/2 cup + 2 T. coconut flour
1 teaspoon orange zest	1/2 cup strawberry "jam"	1/2 cup cocoa powder
1/2 teaspoon salt	1/2 teaspoon salt	
1/2 teaspoon vanilla	1/2 teaspoon vanilla	1/2 teaspoon vanilla
vanilla bean caviar	vanilla bean caviar	

Just a few notes on substitutions and modifications.

The Orange Medallion cookies are the most basic of these three recipes. You could replace the orange zest with lemon zest, or omit altogether. You could add different spices, such as cinnamon and cloves, to give a different flavor.

The Strawberry Medallion cookies have 1/2 cup of cooked-down strawberries; this adds 1/2 cup of wet ingredients. To compensate for this, I reduced the honey, the eggs, and the fats (coconut oil). I used less honey to reduce the wet ingredients and to compensate for the sweetness already added by the strawberry jam. In adding and reducing the wet ingredients, the dough became a bit too sticky and wet, so I added 2 tablespoons of coconut flour for the correct consistency. For this recipe you could substitute the strawberries with any other cooked down fruit (or vegetable, like carrots or pumpkin) to make a totally different cookie flavor.

The Chocolate Medallion cookies include 1/2 cup cocoa powder, which is a dry ingredient (a rather *drying* ingredient, I might add), so I kept the original amounts of honey and oil but increased by one egg. Try adding spearmint or peppermint extract to spice up the chocolate.

Muffins and Quick Breads

Once you've made one kind of muffin or quick bread successfully, it is pretty simple to exchange ingredients and make something else altogether different. Look back to the Banana Nut Muffins recipe and consider these suggestions.

For the bananas, substitute applesauce, other blended fruit or pumpkin, or puréed carrots.

For the coconut oil, substitute butter or palm shortening.

For the walnuts, substitute pecans or macadamia nuts.

If you're using applesauce, add spices appropriate for apple pie, such as cinnamon, nutmeg, and cardamom. If you're using pumpkin, add spices appropriate for pumpkin pie, such as cinnamon, nutmeg, ginger, allspice, and cloves.

If you want to make an item chocolate using cocoa powder, increase the liquids: maybe one more egg, 1/4 cup of applesauce, for each 2-3 tablespoons cocoa powder.

*Once you've made
one kind of muffin
or quick bread
successfully, it is
simple to exchange
ingredients and make
something else
altogether different.*

11. Troubleshooting

Problem: I've created little hockey pucks. How can I salvage botched recipes?

For problematic sweet baked goods:

a. Cube and place in a greased 8" x 8" pan. Add some cut up apples, peaches, pears, or fruit of your choice. Mix an egg or two with a cup of milk and some honey or sweetener of your preference, pour on top of the cubes and allow to sit for a few minutes. Bake at 350°F until a toothpick comes out clean. Here are two recipes for bread pudding to try:

Thai Coconut Bread Pudding with Vanilla Cardamom[11] from All Day I Dream About Food

Gluten-Free Bread Pudding[12] from Mommypotamus

For problematic savory baked goods:

a. Cube the baked good, dry in the oven or dehydrator, and pulse in your food processor to make bread crumbs. Season with your favorite spices and use as a coating to dip pieces of chicken breast. Bake in the oven or fry at a low temperature.

b. Cube and turn into stuffing[13].

c. Toast and liberally spread with butter or mayonnaise and use for sandwiches.

Problem: My batter or dough didn't turn out as expected. I can salvage it but I'm so disappointed.

I find when I have a disaster outcome it helps if I ask myself some questions that may help lead to something new. Would this texture work for pie crust? Would it be better as cookies? Did it crumble

11   Ketchum, Carolyn. (January 10, 2011). Thai Coconut Bread Pudding with Vanilla Cardamom Cream. [Blog Post] Retrieved December 18, 2016 from http://alldayidreamaboutfood.com/2011/01/thai-coconut-bread-pudding-with-vanilla-cardamom-cream-low-carb-and-gluten-free.html

12   Dessinger, Heather. (January 21, 2015). Bread Pudding Recipe. [Blog Post] Retrieved December 18, 2016 from http://www.mommypotamus.com/gluten-free-bread-pudding/

13   Stewart, Starlene. (November 10, 2012) Thanksgiving Menu Planner Review from Heart of Cooking. [Blog Post] Retrieved December 18, 2016 from http://gapsdietjourney.com/2012/11/review-heart-of-cooking-thanksgiving-menu-planner/

into bits? Could it be used as a crumble topping? You may have just discovered a brand new recipe!

Problem: My baked good won't hold together and crumbles to bits when I try to cut it.

This usually indicates the product needs more binder to hold it together—and usually I remedy this with more eggs in the next attempt. Some loaves that crumble when warm from the oven slice perfectly once they have been refrigerated. See the first question on salvaging botched recipes for suggestions on how to use this loaf so you don't waste your ingredients.

Problem: My loaf looks funny and has a weird texture. It almost seems like I baked scrambled eggs.

By chance did you put the batter into the oven before it was done preheating? Or was the oven at a lower temperature than the recipe calls for? This has happened to me. The resulting bread was edible, but as you say, was like a pan of scrambled eggs. Make sure your oven is preheated to the correct temperature next time.

Problem: My muffins spilled out over the edges of the muffin tins.

Keep the batter below the edge of the muffin tin on your next try. Regular wheat flour has a tendency to rise up and keep its form. Since coconut flour is heavier and denser it needs the support of the muffin tins to hold its shape as it bakes.

Problem: My batter didn't rise at all. What went wrong?

Remember that once the vinegar and baking soda meet they begin producing gas bubbles, which causes your product to rise while baking. You must move quickly from the time you begin mixing the vinegar and baking soda together. Always remember to preheat your oven and have the pan you are baking in greased and dusted with coconut flour, or lined with parchment paper, ready for the batter as soon as it is mixed. Then place in the oven to bake right away.

Problem: My loaf was well browned on the outside but soggy in the middle.

This usually indicates that the baking temperature was too high. On your next attempt try lowering the temperature by 25 degrees. You should be able to salvage most of the loaf and the soggy part can be baked in a muffin tin or fried like a pancake. You could also try this recipe as muffins instead of a loaf. Because the dimension is smaller, it will bake quicker and will be less likely to be soggy on the inside.

Problem: My loaf looks great, but when I took a bite my mouth dried out and I almost choked trying to swallow that bite. What happened?

I have found that the batter is in need of more fat when that happens. I have had many beautiful loaves that were firm and cut perfectly but trying to eat them was another matter altogether. The solution I have found has been to add more fat to the batter. If your recipe called for 1/3 cup coconut oil, try another batch using 1/2 cup. There's no need to change amounts of any other ingredients. See the first question for ways to use this loaf.

Problem: My loaf turned green while baking. It tasted perfectly fine, but it grossed my family out and now they don't want to eat coconut flour bread. Why did this happen?

I have had a few occasions where my loaf of bread has turned green while baking and so far the cause remains a mystery. Twice it happened when I was making a savory loaf and omitted honey, so I am a little nervous to not include at least a tablespoon or two of honey in my loaves. Possibly the honey is creating another chemical reaction that prevents the green/gray coloring from happening?

I do have a theory as to why it happens, and I believe it is the same reason why the outer surface of boiled egg yolks sometimes turn green or gray. This occurrence with boiled egg yolks is caused by a chemical reaction due to overcooking[14]. Hydrogen and sulfur react in the egg white to form hydrogen sulfide gas, which in turn reacts with the iron in the egg yolk to form a grayish-green ring where the yolk and white meet.

When it happens with coconut flour loaves, I suspect the green color is due to over baking the loaf since coconut flour baked goods typically use a lot of eggs. My husband once had a loaf that was greenish-gray all the way through, it was pretty gross looking and very browned. From the looks of how brown the crust was, it was definitely baked too long.

My friend Patty from Loving Our Guts has a coconut butter bread recipe[15], which uses coconut cream concentrate and she has several comments from folks whose loaves were greenish. It is definitely something that happens on occasion when baking with coconut flour, but so far I'm not totally certain why. If you know the answer, please get in touch with me so I can update this section!

---

14   Helmenstine, Ph.D., Anne Marie. Why Do Egg Yolks Turn Green? [Blog Post] Retrieved December 18, 2016 from http://chemistry.about.com/od/foodcookingchemistry/f/Why-Do-Egg-Yolks-Turn-Green.htm
15   Lacoss-Arnold, Patricia. (April 27, 2012). Coconut Butter Sandwich Bread [Blog Post] Retrieved December 18, 2016 from http://www.lovingourguts.com/coconut-butter-sandwich-bread/

12. Coconut Flour Recipes Online

Tropical Traditions Gluten-free Coconut Flour Recipes

http://freecoconutrecipes.com/gluten-free-coconut-flour-recipes/

Coconut Flour Recipes

http://www.coconutflourrecipes.org/

Elana's Pantry

http://www.elanaspantry.com/ingredients/coconut-flour/

GAPS Diet Journey

http://gapsdietjourney.com/tag/coconut-flour/

13. About the Author

Starlene Stewart started cooking and baking at the age of 10, when her mother began to assign her some of the kitchen duties. As the oldest of seven children, every meal was like cooking for a small army. Starlene has always experimented with cooking and baking, and finds it a relaxing creative outlet.

Starlene's initial experience with recipe conversion began in her late twenties, when she embarked on the low-fat diet that was all the rage at the time. After a few years of struggling to eat low fat, she learned that our bodies require healthy fats in the foods we eat in order to work properly!

In December 2009, Starlene started blogging to chronicle her experience on the GAPS™ Diet founded by Dr. Natasha Campbell-McBride. She had no idea skills learned 15 years earlier would be so handy in converting old favorite recipes to use coconut flour. Starlene says not every recipe has been a success, but at least 95% are delightful and her family has been very happy with the results. She says some recipes take a second or third or even fourth time to tweak to perfection, but even the "failed" products are edible. Maybe not perfect, but still delicious and made with nutritious ingredients!

If you have any questions or comments about a recipe, or would like to contact Starlene, feel free to send an email to: starlene@gapsdietjourney.com

Find Starlene Online

To find current recipes, please visit Starlene's blog: http://www.gapsdietjourney.com

Starlene's Sales Page: http://www.starlene.com

Starlene's Amazon Author page: https://amazon.com/author/starlene

Facebook: https://www.facebook.com/gapsdietjourney

Twitter: http://www.twitter.com/gapsjourney

YouTube: http://www.youtube.com/conscioustar

Pinterest: http://www.pinterest.com/conscioustar

Blog Talk Radio: http://www.blogtalkradio.com/gapsjourney

Email: starlene@gapsdietjourney.com

Bonus Stand-alone Sample Conversion Sheets

Sign up for my online newsletter Baking with Coconut Flour to get your free bonus Stand-alone Sample Conversion pages. Once signed up you will receive the pages as a PDF document.

As a subscriber you'll receive coupon codes, special announcements, coconut flour baking news and tips, and best of all FREE coconut flour baked goods recipes so you can try out your new baking skills!

Enter this website address into your browser to sign up:

http://gapsdietjourney.com/free-conversion-pages

	Original Recipe Ingredients	Revised Recipe Ingredients
Step 1. 1/4 cup coconut flour for each cup of wheat flour.	2 cups whole wheat flour	1/2 cup coconut flour
Step 2. Weigh the coconut flour; for each ounce use 1 egg -or- if recipe includes mashed fruit or vegetable, advance to Step 3.		5 ounces coconut flour = 5 large eggs
Step 3. If recipe uses 1/2 to 1 cup mashed fruit or vegetable, use 1 egg for every 2 ounces of coconut flour.	1/2 cup bananas	Eggs may be reduced to 2 or 3 instead of 5
Step 4. Substitute half as much honey for white sugar or brown sugar.	1 cup white sugar	1/2 cup honey

Thank you for reading Mastering the Art of Baking with Coconut Flour!

Dear Reader,

I hope you feel much more confident working with this delicious super food! If you have enjoyed reading *Mastering the Art of Baking with Coconut Flour,* I hope you will tell your friends and family, especially those who are curious bakers.

Thank you for helping me spread the word and helping others gain confidence to bake with coconut flour!

Happy Baking!
Starlene
P.S. Feel free to e-mail me at starlene@gapsdietjourney.com with any questions, comments or suggestions. I would really love to hear from you!

Upcoming Titles from Starlene D. Stewart

Baker's Dozen Quick Savory Breads, Volume 5 in the Coconut Flour Baked Goods series will include delicious savory breads like Six Seed Brown Bread, Bacon & Onion, Spinach & Walnut, and Goat Cheese and Kalamata Olives.

Made in the USA
Columbia, SC
16 February 2020